Exclusively

FIRST LADIES

TRIVIA

by Anthony S. Pitch

Mino Publications

Published by

Mino Publications
9009 Paddock Lane
Potomac, MD 20854

Library of Congress Catalog Card No. 85-60254

ISBN 0-931719-03-8

Printed in the United States of America

For Marion, with love

Also by Anthony S. Pitch

Exclusively Presidential Trivia
Exclusively Washington Trivia
Washington D.C. Sightseers Guide
Bazak Guide to Israel
Bazak Guide to Italy
Peace
Inside Zambia - And Out

Exclusively First Ladies Trivia is available at special bulk purchase discounts for sales promotions, conventions, fund raisers or premiums.

For details, write to

Mino Publications
9009 Paddock Lane
Potomac, MD 20854

QUESTIONS

1. When she was a child this tomboy beat up a neighborhood boy.

2. Why did Edith Roosevelt sit through a comedy after learning her husband had been shot?

3. Who moved home 35 times in 35 years?

4. This First Lady's son won the Congressional Medal of Honor.

5. Which future First Lady honeymooned aboard a ship bound for China?

6. This First Lady was a 9th generation descendant of the Indian, Pocahontas.

7. Why did Martha Washington cut up her husband's Continental Army uniform?

8. What did Jacqueline Kennedy give LBJ for Christmas 1963?

9. How did Ulysses Grant and his wife, Julia, address each other?

10. Unknown to each other these two future First Ladies were at Smith College at the same time.

ANSWERS

1. Betty Bloomer Ford

2. She didn't think it was serious because he gave his scheduled speech

3. Mamie Eisenhower

4. Lucy Hayes' son, Webb, in the Philippines, 1899

5. Lou Hoover

6. Edith Bolling Wilson

7. She used a piece of the material to make herself a satin drawstring bag

8. A book entitled *The Inauguration Addresses from George Washington to John F. Kennedy.*

9. She called him *Ulys*; he called her *Mrs. G.*

10. Nancy Reagan and Barbara Bush

QUESTIONS

11. Who brought the first piano into the White House?

12. Which First Lady and her husband read Shakespeare to each other?

13. What was Mary Todd Lincoln's nickname before her marriage?

14. How many guests did Helen and William Howard Taft invite to their 25th wedding anniversary party?

15. Whose German shepherd bit the Prime Minister of Canada?

16. How many servants did Elizabeth Monroe have when her husband was U.S. envoy in Paris?

17. What did Rachel Jackson have in common with Abigail Fillmore?

18. Why did Jane Pierce refuse to give birth to her third son in Washington D.C.?

19. What wisecrack was inscribed on the sundial in Bess Truman's home in Independence, Missouri?

ANSWERS

11. Abigail Adams

12. Lucretia and James Garfield

13. *Molly*

14. 5,000

15. Eleanor Roosevelt's

16. A cook, gardener, coachman and 4 other domestics

17. They both taught their husbands — future Presidents — to write English

18. She had lost 2 sons and did not want to risk giving birth in the capital's unhealthy climate

19. *My Face Marks the Sunny Hours, What Can You Say of Yours?*

20. What was Grace Coolidge doing the day before she unexpectedly became First Lady?

21. Whose racial prejudices made her recoil when watching the play, *Othello*?

22. By what approximate amount did Martha Custis enrich George Washington on their marriage?

23. How soon after giving birth did Pat Nixon resume campaigning for RMN's 1946 Congressional candidacy?

24. What did the child, Frances Folsom, call Grover Cleveland, long before their marriage?

25. Austerely religious, she appeared at her husband's inauguration dressed in black.

26. Who manufactured Edith Bolling Wilson's sewing machine?

27. Orphaned as a pre-teen, this woman presided as First Lady when her bachelor uncle became President.

ANSWERS

20. Raking wood chips off the lawn at Plymouth Notch, Vermont

21. Abigail Adams admitted feeling *"horror"* whenever Othello touched Desdemona

22. $100,000

23. 3 weeks

24. *Uncle Cleve*

25. Sarah Polk

26. Wilcox and Gibbs

27. Harriet Lane

QUESTIONS

28. Who was Lady Bird Johnson's admitted favorite President - aside from her husband?

29. While they were courting he gave her 2 volumes of *The Geology of the State of New York.*

30. What color was Dolley Madison's White House bathtub?

31. Who prayed regularly that her husband would not become President?

32. Which foreign leader gave Jacqueline Kennedy the gift of a horse, *Sardar?*

33. Why was Rosalynn Carter tearful when the Shah of Iran spoke on the White House lawn?

34. What was Lucretia Garfield doing at Elberon, N.J. when her husband was shot by an assassin?

35. What did the Secret Service select as Nancy Reagan's code name?

36. Which First Lady was terrified of flying in planes?

ANSWERS

28. Thomas Jefferson

29. William Howard Taft gave these to Helen Herron because geology was one of her favorite subjects

30. Green

31. Margaret "Peggy" Taylor, wife of Zachary Taylor, 12th President

32. Pakistani President Ayub Khan

33. She was affected by tear gas thrown to break up a melée of the Shah's supporters and opponents beyond the fence

34. Convalescing from a severe attack of malaria

35. *Rainbow*

36. Mamie Eisenhower

37. Whom did Harry Truman laud as *First Lady of the World*?

38. Which First Lady had a pet parrot?

39. What was Mary Todd Lincoln's favorite form of entertainment?

40. Why was water from the Jordan River taken to the White House?

41. Why did Florence Harding extend her left hand to greet visitors?

42. What were the favorite pastimes of Abigail Adams?

43. Who ran sobbing down a hotel corridor after her husband lost the Presidential election?

44. Name the woman married on March 17, her mother's birthday.

45. Who gave herself 4 stars for her handling of the visit of the Queen of England?

46. How did the congregation at Mary and Abraham Lincoln's church show them respect?

ANSWERS

37. Eleanor Roosevelt

38. Dolley Madison

39. The opera

40. For the baptism of First Lady Caroline Harrison's granddaughter, Mary McKee

41. Her right hand was swollen from greeting 7,000 guests at the New Year's Day reception, 1922

42. Reading and writing letters

43. Pat Nixon in 1960

44. Eleanor Roosevelt

45. Betty Ford

46. They stood up when they walked in. But they didn't allow the Lincoln's to leave first

47. Why did Frances Cleveland ban the public from the south grounds of the White House?

48. Who was older—Martha or George Washington?

49. From whom did Lady Bird Johnson learn that Presidential assassin, Lee Harvey Oswald, had been murdered?

50. What was Lucy Hayes doing when she suffered the stroke that killed her 3 days later?

51. Which First Lady saw a German Zeppelin bomber shot down over London, England?

52. Of what disease did Abigail Adams' daughter, "Nabby", die?

53. What was the Secret Service code name for Bess Truman during World War II?

54. The wrap-around skirt of this First Lady fell to the floor after her meeting with a female reporter.

55. Where was Grace Coolidge when President Coolidge died?

ANSWERS

47. Because so many people would pat and peck her new-born baby, Ruth

48. Martha was eight months older

49. From Eunice Shriver, sister of the slain President

50. Sewing

51. Lou Hoover

52. Cancer, after a mastectomy 2 years earlier

53. *Fernlake*

54. Nancy Reagan. It happened in the private living quarters of the White House

55. Out shopping in their hometown of Northampton, Mass. while he was at home

56. Which aging former First Lady crossed the Atlantic in the same ship as actress Sarah Bernhardt?

57. Why did President McKinley breach protocol by having his wife, Ida, sit next to him at official dinners?

58. Which First Lady campaigned unsuccessfully for the erection of a new and larger White House?

59. For what purpose did Mamie Eisenhower get together so often with women friends?

60. Why did Jacqueline Kennedy's sister, Lee Radziwill, miss the inauguration of President Kennedy?

61. What was the value of the estate of Mary Todd Lincoln, who thought she was a pauper?

62. Why did Helen Taft get rid of her cow grazing on the White House grounds?

63. What gesture by Pat Nixon so charmed Premier Chou En-lai in China?

ANSWERS

56. Mary Todd Lincoln

57. Because she was prone to epileptic seizures

58. Caroline Harrison, wife of Benjamin Harrison

59. To play card games

60. She had recently given birth to a daughter in England

61. Almost $90,000

62. She exchanged it for one which produced more milk

63. She curtsied when they met

64. How long was Frances Folsom's dress train at her marriage to Grover Cleveland?

65. What human tragedy had similar elements for Jane Pierce and Mary Todd Lincoln?

66. This religiously austere First Lady banned card-playing in the White House.

67. A painting by this French impressionist hung in Rosalynn and Jimmy Carter's White House bedroom.

68. This First Lady's father had the names of a former President.

69. In 1851 he said: "I love you." She replied: "I like you very well." They were married 14 months later.

70. Who pressured Congress into approving funds for the first White House library?

71. This First Lady fulfilled a teen-age vow to marry a man *"destined to be President"*.

72. Who was satirized by the media as *the lovely Lady Presidentess* because of her opulent style?

ANSWERS

64. 15 ft.

65. Each had a son who died at the age of 11

66. Sarah Polk

67. Paul Cézanne

68. Lady Bird Johnson's father was Thomas Jefferson Taylor

69. Lucy Webb and Rutherford Hayes

70. Former schoolteacher then First Lady, Abigail Fillmore

71. Helen Taft

72. Julia Tyler, second wife of the 10th President

73. Which future President told his wife-to-be that he loved his country more than her?

74. What was the name of the home where newly-marrieds Martha and George Washington lived for 3 months?

75. Who was the first widow of a Chief Executive to benefit from Secret Service protection for life?

76. What music did Edith Kermit Roosevelt request for her funeral?

77. Who were *Rob Roy* and *Prudence Prim*?

78. What was the title of Eleanor Roosevelt's syndicated daily newspaper column?

79. At what hour of the morning did Abigail Adams regularly get up?

80. How did Julia Grant unwittingly save Ulysses Grant from harm the night Lincoln was shot?

81. What home-State food did Bess Truman serve for Princess Elizabeth of England?

ANSWERS

73. John Quincy Adams confessed this to Louisa Catherine Johnson

74. *The White House*

75. Mamie Eisenhower

76. Choral sections of Beethoven's 9th Symphony

77. Grace Coolidge's white Collies

78. *My Day*

79. 5 a.m.

80. She had turned down Lincoln's invitation to join him at Ford's Theater

81. Baked Old Missouri Ham

82. From what birth defect did Mary Todd Lincoln's son, Tad, suffer?

83. Who forbade uniforms of any kind for White House staff?

84. How did Edith Bolling Wilson come to rename more than 7 dozen German ships?

85. Why did Eleanor Roosevelt sleep in her White House maid's ironing room?

86. How much did Elizabeth and James Monroe pay for their diplomatic residence in Paris?

87. When was the last occasion Lady Bird Johnson flew aboard *Air Force One* with LBJ?

88. What did Jacqueline Kennedy give her children's English nannie after 7 years service?

89. Where did First Lady Harriet Lane take the British Prince of Wales after a White House reception?

ANSWERS

82. He had a speech impediment because of a cleft palate

83. Caroline Harrison

84. The government sequestered them in U.S. ports during World War I

85. She gave up her own room after inviting too many guests for an inauguration

86. Approximately $15,000

87. 1972—when she accompanied his body to Texas after the lying-in-state in Washington, D.C.

88. An inscribed, leather-bound family album

89. To a game of ten-pins with pupils at a girls' school

90. Which two First Ladies would not sit at a table set for 13?

91. Where did Frances Cleveland buy her trousseau?

92. This First Lady's son took along the book, *Treasure Island*, in case he was bored during his father's inauguration.

93. For how long did Julia and Ulysses Grant travel around the world after leaving the White House?

94. What was unique about Grace Coolidge's inheritance from her husband?

95. Who was First Lady when White House china was ordered from an American manufacturer for the first time?

96. What sum did Congress vote for Anna Harrison, whose husband died after a month as President?

97. This First Lady spoke French before English because her nurse was a French woman.

ANSWERS

90. Lou Hoover and Eleanor Roosevelt

91. In Paris, France

92. Helen Taft's youngest son, Charles

93. 26 months

94. He left everything to her in a one-sentence will — the shortest made by any President

95. Edith Bolling Wilson. It was made by Lenox, Inc. of Trenton, N.J.

96. $25,000

97. Eleanor Roosevelt

98. Whose daughter eloped with Jefferson Davis but died of fever 3 months later?

99. What was so personal about Mamie Eisenhower's bracelets?

100. This First Lady's features reminded a visting Briton of *"Spanish donnas"*.

101. What was the monthly wage bill paid by Edith Kermit Roosevelt for her 10 servants in 1890?

102. Who were the two outstandingly popular First Ladies?

103. What did President Jackson wear in memory of his wife, Rachel?

104. Where did John and Jacqueline Kennedy honeymoon?

105. Which First Lady was on a salt-free diet?

106. She wrote a book about her cocker spaniel to raise money to campaign against illiteracy

107. What did First Lady Elizabeth Monroe serve at her fortnightly receptions?

ANSWERS

98. Sarah, daughter of Margaret and Zachary Taylor

99. They included charms to mark special events in her life

100. Sarah Polk

101. $210

102. Dolley Madison and Frances Cleveland

103. A miniature portrait suspended around his neck by a black cord

104. Acapulco, Mexico

105. Bess Truman

106. Barbara Bush

107. Wine, tea, coffee and iced cakes

QUESTIONS

108. Who found out after 25 years of marriage that her husband didn't like anything for breakfast?

109. What was Florence Harding's nickname?

110. Why was Dolley Madison banished from Quaker Meetings?

111. Which First Lady studied speed-reading with her husband?

112. Who made Eleanor Roosevelt's personal typewriter?

113. This First Lady's only son fought for the South in the Civil War.

114. Guess who wrote that *"time was given for use, not waste"?*

115. Which First Lady was a part-time bank teller supporting herself through college?

116. How long were Bess and Harry Truman married?

117. Where did Jacqueline Bouvier (Kennedy) study abroad in her junior year at Vassar?

ANSWERS

108. Rosalynn Carter

109. *Duchess*

110. Because of her marriage to Episcopalian, James Madison

111. Rosalynn Carter

112. L.C. Smith & Corona Typewriters, Inc.

113. Margaret Taylor's son, Richard, whose father, Zachary, was President 1849-50

114. Abigail Adams

115. Pat Ryan Nixon

116. 53 years

117. The Sorbonne in Paris, France

118. Who decorated the White House living quarters in an oriental style?

119. Who read in the paper that her husband had died in battle, then received a telegram to the contrary?

120. Nathaniel Hawthorne looked at this former First Lady in her coffin and thought she looked like a carved image.

121. What is unique about the White House portrait of Eleanor Roosevelt?

122. Whose complexion was said to be beautiful because she ate arsenic?

123. How much older than President Fillmore was his first wife, Abigail?

124. Who gave birth to her only child 4 days after her 39th birthday?

125. Why did Mamie Eisehower have to rest in bed so much?

126. How long after President Taylor was buried did his wife, Margaret, move out of the White House?

ANSWERS

118. Helen Taft

119. Lucy Hayes, during the Civil War

120. Jane Pierce, whose husband, Franklin, was Hawthorne's friend from college days

121. It is the only portrait of her painted from life

122. This was the outrageous claim about Frances Cleveland by a merchant in arsenic

123. 22 months

124. Bess Truman

125. She had a rheumatic heart condition

126. That same day

QUESTIONS

127. Which First Lady was responsible for buying the portrait of Martha Washington, by Eliphalet Andrews, for the East Room?

128. Why couldn't Abraham Lincoln stay by his wife's bedside when she was hospitalized after a carriage accident?

129. Who translated Plato's works with her sons?

130. President Garfield's wife's first name was Lucretia. What did he call her?

131. What did Queen Victoria's son give First Lady Harriet Lane after staying at the White House?

132. How did Edith Bolling Wilson get a piece of the German truce flag from World War I?

133. At large receptions Edith Kermit Roosevelt usually refrained from doing this.

134. How was Elizabeth Monroe's health impaired when she attended Napoleon's coronation?

ANSWERS

127. Lucy Hayes

128. It happened during the battle at Gettysburg

129. Louisa Catherine Adams

130. *Crete*

131. A set of engravings of the British Royal Family

132. French Premier, Georges Clemenceau, gave it to her

133. Shaking hands with the guests

134. She became rheumatic from the cold in Notre Dame Cathedral

135. How many of Mary Todd Lincoln's four sons died in childhood?

136. This couple did not own a car until he became Vice President.

137. A stickler for tidiness, this First Lady objected to her husband allowing the dog to lie on the furniture.

138. How many vacation trips to Europe did Helen and William Howard Taft take before she gave birth to their first child?

139. What time did Julia and Ulyssess Grant regularly breakfast with their children?

140. Where is Gilbert Stuart's famous oil painting of Dolley Madison?

141. How tall was Abigail Adams?

142. What was unique about Nancy Reagan's first inaugural gown?

143. A mourning President sat for two nights beside the body of this First Lady.

144. The birthdays of this woman's children fell within two days of each other. Name all three persons.

ANSWERS

135. Three: Eddie, Tad, Willie

136. Grace and Calvin Coolidge

137. Pat Nixon

138. Two

139. 8:30 a.m.

140. At Philadelphia, in the Pennsylvania Academy of the Fine Arts

141. Just over 5 ft.

142. Alone among her predecessors, she bared a shoulder completely

143. Woodrow Wilson mourned thus over his first wife, Ellen

144. Jacqueline Kennedy's children, John, Jr., born November 25th, and his sister, Caroline, born November 27th

145. Name the former Associated Press writer who lived in the White House as Eleanor Roosevelt's friend.

146. How many times had Rosalynn Carter visited the White House before she became First Lady?

147. Who bought radio station *KTBC* with a cash inheritance from her mother's estate?

148. How did George Washington begin the letter to his wife informing her he would be commanding the Continental Army?

149. Five of this woman's 10 children died before she became First Lady.

150. Who was the bride of the first President to marry in office?

151. Which First Lady crocheted a bed spread for the White House?

152. Why did Betty and Gerald Ford marry on a Friday?

153. What was Rosalynn Carter's given first name?

ANSWERS

145. Ms. Lorena "Hick" Hickok

146. Three times

147. Lady Bird Johnson. The purchase of the Austin, Tx. station was approved in 1943

148. "*My Dearest*....."

149. Anna Symmes Harrison, 1775-1864

150. Julia Gardiner Tyler

151. Grace Coolidge

152. So they could watch a college football game on Saturday

153. Eleanor

154. Who said: *"I have only one real hobby—it's my husband."*?

155. Together with her husband, this linguist spent 5 years translating a 16th century textbook on mining from Latin to English.

156. By what names did Abraham and Mary Todd Lincoln call each other?

157. Where was Helen Taft when she suffered a stroke after only 2 months as First Lady?

158. This woman was once the only female student at Ohio Wesleyan University in Delaware, Ohio.

159. How many fireplaces had to be lit daily to rid the White House of dampness during Abigail Adams' stay?

160. This First Lady was the first President General of the National Society of the Daughters of the American Revolution.

161. What did Rachel Jackson whisper before her death, only weeks after her husband's election as President?

ANSWERS

154. Florence Harding

155. Lou and Herbert Hoover

156. She called him *father* and he called her *mother*

157. Aboard the Presidential yacht, *Mayflower,* on the Potomac River

158. Lucy Hayes

159. 13

160. Caroline Harrison, wife of Benjamin Harrison

161. *"I'd rather be a doorkeeper in the House of God than live in that palace at Washington."*

QUESTIONS

162. Which First Lady yielded to pressure from her husband not to have corrective surgery for her crossed eyes?

163. Why did Eleanor Roosevelt often sit before the statue of a woman called *Grief* in a Washington D.C. cemetery?

164. Why did the band play *He's Going to Marry Yum-Yum* when President Cleveland reviewed a Memorial Day parade?

165. How did Rosalynn Carter briefly steal the limelight at Egyptian-Israeli peace talks at Camp David, Md.?

166. What words did Abraham Lincoln have engraved on the wedding ring he gave Mary Todd?

167. How much did Edith Kermit Roosevelt pay her social secretary?

168. Why was Grace Coolidge known as *The First Lady of Baseball?*

169. What color dress did the dying Martha Washington select to be buried in?

ANSWERS

162. Julia Grant—after he said he liked her eyes crossed

163. She said it brought her out of the doldrums

164. He was engaged to be married 3 days later to Frances Folsom—27 years his junior

165. She proposed a prayer for peace

166. *Love Is Eternal*

167. A starting salary of $1,400 a year

168. Because she was a baseball buff

169. White

170. Whose father died from inhaling carbon monoxide while fixing a car?

171. Name the future First Lady who co-founded a chapter of Pi Beta Phi fraternity at the University of Vermont.

172. At whose weekly evening concerts in the White House did pianist Jan Paderewski perform?

173. Why was Nancy Reagan afraid of locked doors?

174. What did Dolley Madison order carried away from the White House *after* saving Washington's portrait from advancing British troops?

175. Which First Lady was once married to an alcoholic who died aged 35?

176. Her fiancé painted her name on his World War II warplane.

177. Where did Jacqueline Bouvier meet John Kennedy?

178. Why was oxygen administered to Rosalynn Carter in Quito, Ecuador?

ANSWERS

170. Betty Ford's—when she was 16

171. Grace Coolidge

172. Those organized by Edith Kermit Roosevelt

173. Once her biological father locked her in

174. A framed draft of the *Declaration of Independence*

175. Florence Harding (formerly DeWolfe)

176. Barbara Bush's aviator fiancé, George

177. At dinner in the home of Charles Bartlett, Washington correspondent for the Chattanooga *Times* (1952)

178. Because of the effects of the high altitude—almost 2 miles above sea level

QUESTIONS

179. Which First Lady ordered nightly illumination of the White House?

180. Which future First Lady covered the coronation of Britain's Queen Elizabeth as a photographer for the Washington *Times-Herald*?

181. Who unwittingly committed bigamy?

182. How high off the ground was Grace Coolidge's shortest dress?

183. Was Betty Ford in favor of a pardon for Richard Nixon?

184. Who took ice cold morning showers or baths from childhood?

185. Why did Martha Washington write a letter to President Adams on the last day of 1799?

186. Why did some observers mistakenly think Mamie Eisenhower was often tipsy?

187. What did guests shower Dolley and James Madison with at their wedding?

188. How many of Mary Todd Lincoln's close kin died for the Confederacy?

ANSWERS

179. Pat Nixon

180. Jacqueline Bouvier (Kennedy)

181. Rachel and Andrew Jackson thought her first husband had obtained a divorce but it came through only after they married

182. 10½″

183. Yes

184. Eleanor Roosevelt

185. She agreed to the burial of her husband under an intended monument in Washington

186. She had Ménières disease which affected the inner ear and her sense of balance

187. Flowers and rice

188. Two brothers and the husband of her sister

189. She was the daughter of a State Senator, granddaughter of a Congressman, and wife of a President.

190. What gift did James Polk give his wife, Sarah, to celebrate his inauguration?

191. Name the first First Lady born in the 20th century.

192. This lady said she had such faith in her husband that *"if he told me I would die tomorrow at 10 o'clock, I would believe him."*

193. Why was Jane Pierce described as *"the very picture of melancholy"*?

194. What was Martha Washington's maiden name?

195. Who was the first South Carolinian to be First Lady?

196. Why was Edith Kermit Roosevelt excluded from the State dinner for Prince Henry, brother of the German Emperor?

197. Where did young marrieds, Rosalynn and Jimmy Carter, dream of retiring to?

ANSWERS

189. Helen Taft

190. Portraits of his predecessors painted on a fan

191. Jacqueline Kennedy—July 28th, 1929

192. Grace Coolidge

193. She never got over witnessing the death of her son, 11, crushed in a train derailment

194. Dandridge

195. Angelica Van Buren, daughter-in-law of widower President Martin Van Buren

196. No women were invited to the White House dinner in 1902

197. Hawaii

198. How many First Ladies have appeared on U.S. postage stamps?

199. Why was Abigail Adams carried into her Massachusetts home after leaving Washington as First Lady?

200. A compulsive shopper, this woman was criticized by the media for having *"ransacked the treasures of the Broadway dry goods stores."*

201. After this First Lady died, her husband married her niece.

202. How many lines did Betty Ford use to cross the *t*s in her signature?

203. Why did Lucy Hayes put on her wedding dress 25 years later?

204. What drew Jacqueline Kennedy Onassis to the White House for the first time since 1963?

205. Why did Lady Bird Johnson and LBJ make a gift of a 19th century mailbox to the Japanese Premier?

ANSWERS

198. Four—Martha Washington, Dolley Madison, Eleanor Roosevelt, Abigail Adams.

199. She had injured her foot in a hole in the floor of her carriage

200. Mary Todd Lincoln

201. Caroline Harrison's niece, Mary Dimmick, married Benjamin Harrison

202. One

203. For a repeat wedding ceremony

204. In 1971 she accepted Pat Nixon's invitation to a private viewing of the new portraits of herself and JFK

205. He had once been Postmaster General of Japan

QUESTIONS

206. How did Julia Grant always prepare for unexpected guests?

207. What did Secret Servicemen beat to death in front of Grace Coolidge?

208. In which country did Louisa Catherine Adams give birth to her first child?

209. How much money did James Madison pay out to settle the debts of Dolley Madison's profligate son by her first marriage?

210. Which First Lady had her paintings included in an exhibition of renowned female painters?

211. How did the Reagans get to own *Lady,* a Belgian Shepherd?

212. Why did Secretary of State James Madison work at Dolley Madison's bedside in 1805?

213. What was the family connection between Jacqueline Kennedy and a former president of the Polish Red Cross?

ANSWERS

206. She prepared half a dozen extra places at the dinner table

207. A 4 ft. long gopher snake as she prepared for a hike

208. Berlin, Germany

209. $20,000

210. Ellen Wilson

211. She was brought to them after being thrown from an auto

212. She had an ulcerated tumor on a leg

213. Prince Janusz Radziwill was father of the man who married Jacqueline Kennedy's sister

214. Which First Lady was criticized for the formal nod of her head when visitors bowed before her?

215. What did President Eisenhower do with the White House room used as private offices by Eleanor Roosevelt and Bess Truman?

216. Did Pat Nixon interview the women short-listed to be her social secretary?

217. Whose first visit to the White House was with her class of deaf mute pupils?

218. What was Edith Bolling Wilson's bath made of in her suite at Buckingham Palace, London?

219. What did Soviet Foreign Minister Gromyko urge Nancy Reagan to whisper nightly in her husband's ear?

220. What gift did JFK make to Edith Bolling Wilson?

221. How did Calvin Coolidge propose marriage to Grace Goodhue?

ANSWERS

214. Elizabeth Monroe

215. He used it as his private room to paint in

216. No. She asked that John Ehrlichman do it

217. Grace Coolidge

218. Marble

219. The word *peace*

220. The pen with which he signed authorization for a commission to design a memorial to Woodrow Wilson

221. He said: *"I am going to be married to you."*

222. How long did Florence Harding talk to her deceased husband as his open coffin lay in the White House?

223. This outdoor type would stroll or horse-ride regardless of the weather.

224. The father of this First Lady committed suicide by shooting himself in the head.

225. How many people saw Jacqueline Kennedy's guided tour of the White House over network TV?

226. Guess which male Abigail Adams referred to as *"one of the choicest ones of the earth."*?

227. What kind of dancing did Rosalynn Carter organize for a White House picnic for Congresspersons?

228. A month before her husband's inauguration as Veep, Edith Kermit Roosevelt studied which foreign language?

229. Was Bess Truman in favor of her husband running for another term in 1952?

ANSWERS

222. For more than an hour

223. Edith Kermit Roosevelt

224. Bess Truman's father, at the age of 43

225. More than 56 million

226. Thomas Jefferson

227. Square dancing

228. German

229. Absolutely against

230. What did Betty Ford say to Richard Nixon as he left the White House in disgrace?

231. Why did Harry Truman tell his pilot to swoop over the White House when Bess was there?

232. How did Eleanor Roosevelt react when the Colony Club of New York black-balled the Jewish wife of the Secretary of the Treasury?

233. It took her almost a decade to needlepoint a 140 sq. ft. rug

234. Why did Jacqueline Kennedy cherish two maple chairs donated to the White House?

235. How heavy is the granite slab over the remains of Florence Harding?

236. This First Lady's grandson was a deaf mute.

237. What was the value of the estate President Taft left his wife, Helen?

ANSWERS

230. *"Have a nice trip"*

231. To prove to his skeptical wife that flying was safe

232. She resigned from the club

233. Barbara Bush

234. They were made in 1820 by her great-great grandfather, Michel Bouvier, a French immigrant cabinetmaker

235. Two tons

236. Elizabeth Monroe

237. $475,000 including their homes in Washington D.C. and Murray Bay, Quebec, Canada

238. How many pounds of turkey were served at the inaugural ball for James and Lucretia Garfield?

239. What did *à la Cleveland* mean to Washington women in vogue?

240. Who bought presents throughout the year and squirrelled them away in a *Christmas closet?*

241. What was the cost of the 1,000 pieces of chinaware ordered by Lucy Hayes from Haviland, France?

242. President Taft was a Unitarian and his wife Episcopalean. What church did their children belong to?

243. Where was Bess Truman when Puerto Ricans tried to assassinate HST at Blair House?

244. How much older than her husband was Florence Harding?

245. Which First Lady brought the first twin beds into the White House?

ANSWERS

238. 1,500 lbs.

239. Copying Frances Cleveland's hairstyle, by forming a knot at the nape of the neck

240. Eleanor Roosevelt

241. $15,000

242. Their mother's

243. Dressing in an adjoining bedroom

244. 5 years

245. Helen Taft

246. What rental did newly-weds Jane and Congressman Franklin Pierce pay for a rocking chair?

247. Which First Lady was sometimes addressed—unsolicited—as *Your Majesty*?

248. What did Julia Grant forever call her husband after his capture of Vicksburg?

249. Which First Lady was her husband's 5th cousin?

250. Who accompanied newly-marrieds President John Tyler and his wife, Julia, on their honeymoon?

251. Louisa Catherine Adams' paternal uncle was Governor of which state?

252. On what single occasion did Letitia Tyler, an invalid, act as official hostess in the White House?

253. This First Lady was opposed to women's suffrage but her daughter became an activist in the movement.

254. Which First Lady publicly denied that the President had cruelly mistreated her?

ANSWERS

246. $1.50 per Congressional session

247. Martha Washington, by women attending receptions in Philadelphia

248. *Victor*

249. Eleanor Roosevelt

250. The bride's sister, Margaret—not an unusual custom of the mid-19th century

251. Thomas Johnson was Governor of Maryland

252. At the wedding of her daughter, Elizabeth, in 1842

253. Helen Taft's daughter, Professor Helen Manning

254. Frances Cleveland, after a spate of unfounded rumors

255. This First Lady endeared herself to foreign audiences in fluent French, Spanish and Italian.

256. Who put her old dresses up for sale in New York City?

257. Why did the elderly Dolley Madison wear a veil over her face?

258. Which incumbent President referred to his wife in public as *First Mama*?

259. Why did Lady Bird Johnson get down on her hands and knees in Washington, D.C.'s Mall?

260. What diplomatic post did Louisa Adams' father hold when she first met John Quincy Adams?

261. Why did Julia Grant threaten to withhold a servant's wages and use the money to buy him a house?

262. Why did Frances Cleveland tell the White House staff to leave everything as she had arranged it—even though her husband's term was up?

ANSWERS

255. Jacqueline Kennedy

256. Mary Todd Lincoln, erroneously believing she was almost destitute. Only a few were sold

257. She had a prolonged eye infection

258. Gerald Ford and his wife, Betty, during the 1976 Presidential campaign

259. To plant pansies

260. American Consul in London, England

261. Because she knew real estate values would soar and he would soon be unable to afford a home

262. She said she would return as First Lady—and she did, 4 years later

263. Why did Theodore Roosevelt throw his niece, Eleanor, into the pool?

264. Why did White House staff call it *The Pink Palace*?

265. Though normally stingy, President Coolidge was almost profligate when it came to spending money for........?

266. Why did Elizabeth Monroe cause such a furor among Washington society?

267. What movie did Pat and Richard Nixon view within 48 hours of moving into the White House?

268. How did Helen Taft break with tradition on Inauguration Day 1909?

269. Of whom was it said she had *"the brains of Scarlett O'Hara and the charm of Dolley Madison."*?

270. This First Lady's father was a British Army captain before becoming an American.

271. Who regularly took shorthand notes on her travels?

ANSWERS

263. *"Horrified"* that she couldn't swim, he wanted her to learn the hard way

264. Because Mamie Eisenhower had a mania for pink

265. His wife's clothes

266. She announced that while she would receive visitors, she would not visit at their homes

267. *The Shoes of the Fisherman*

268. She rode back with her husband after his inauguration

269. Lady Bird Johnson

270. Elizabeth Kortright Monroe

271. Lady Bird Johnson

272. What was the first car owned by Pat and Richard Nixon?

273. How much did Dolley Madison pay for a slave, after insisting the slave be freed after 5 years?

274. Why did Secretary of State William Evarts refuse to allow the Diplomatic Corps to their annual dinner at the White House?

275. Who kept caged canaries in her bedroom?

276. What color was Martha Washington's formal porcelain service?

277. From what illness did Jane Pierce suffer?

278. What time did Julia and Ulysses Grant normally go to bed?

279. With whom did Bess and Harry Truman lodge after their honeymoon?

280. What did Lady Bird Johnson feature on her state china service?

281. This woman continued playing solitaire as a shell blew out her front door during the Boxer Rebellion in China.

ANSWERS

272. An Oldsmobile

273. $400

274. Because First Lady Lucy Hayes had banned liquor and wine

275. Grace Coolidge

276. White

277. Tuberculosis

278. 9:30–10 p.m.

279. Her mother and grandmother

280. Wildflowers native to the U.S.

281. Lou Hoover

QUESTIONS

282. Guess whose ice cream plates featured decorations resembling snowshoes?

283. Which future First Lady carried passport no. 218793 in 1948?

284. How old was Martha Washington when she sat for the famous portrait by Gilbert Stuart?

285. Why did Julia Tyler wear a gold pen as a pendant on her husband's last day as President?

286. How much did Mary Todd Lincoln over-spend on White House redecorations in 1861?

287. How many miles did Pat Nixon log in travel abroad while First Lady?

288. Which First Lady hung up her laundry to dry in the White House East Room?

289. How long were Edith and Woodrow Wilson engaged before their marriage?

290. Which First Lady confessed to seeing her dead son frequently at her bedside?

ANSWERS

282. Lucy Hayes' White House service

283. Jacqueline Lee Bouvier

284. 65

285. He had used it the day before to sign legislation admitting Texas to the Union

286. About $7,000

287. Almost 109,000 miles

288. Abigail Adams—because the mansion was still being built

289. 3 months

290. Mary Todd Lincoln

291. Who was First Lady for the briefest time?

292. Who selected her school contemporary as her husband's White House press secretary?

293. A voracious reader, she could manage a book a day.

294. This First Lady was among only a handful of women whom Japanese diplomats agreed to meet.

295. How did Grace Coolidge get around her husband's warning not to make speeches?

296. How old was Martha Dandridge (Washington) when she married her first husband?

297. Why did Mary Todd Lincoln try and poison herself?

298. Why did Nancy Reagan's son drop out of Yale?

299. What was the Secret Service code name for Betty Ford?

ANSWERS

291. Anna Symmes Harrison, wife of the 9th President, who died after a month in office

292. Bess Truman suggested, and HST approved their mutual school contemporary, Charlie Ross

293. Barbara Bush

294. Harriet Lane, niece of President Buchanan

295. She used sign language

296. 17

297. Because in 1875 a court heard evidence by her son of her insanity

298. Ron Reagan, Jr. dropped out to join the Joffrey Ballet

299. *Pinafore*

300. Guess who sent a Christmas card every year to her former London parlor maid?

301. Who destroyed nearly all the letters George Washington wrote to his wife?

302. Why was Louisa Adams not at the side of her husband, John Quincy, when he died?

303. How old was Pat Ryan when she married Richard Nixon?

304. Why did Frances Cleveland enter the history books when she gave birth to a daughter in 1893?

305. This First Lady's inaugural gown was based on her own sketches and ideas.

306. What tree did Grace Coolidge have planted at the White House in memory of her son, Calvin, Jr.?

307. What was Florence Harding's gift to her husband on his 55th birthday—the day he was elected President?

308. How did Edith Bolling Galt begin letters to Woodrow Wilson during his courtship of her?

ANSWERS

300. Lou Hoover

301. His wife, Matha, shortly before she died in 1802

302. He collapsed in the Capitol, Washington D.C., didn't recognize her when she arrived, and she was asked to leave the room with all other women

303. 28

304. It was the first time an incumbent President's child had been born in the White House

305. Jacqueline Kennedy

306. A Vermont spruce

307. A surprise birthday party with a cake and pink candles

308. *"My Precious One"*

309. Where did Rosalynn and Jimmy Carter relax for a few days after his 1980 electoral defeat?

310. What names was Nancy Reagan given at birth?

311. Why were Russian Grand Dukes Alexis and Constantin the last persons to be served wine in a 4-year span at the White House?

312. How many buttons did Jacqueline Kennedy invariably have on her long pairs of gloves?

313. What jobs did Eleanor Roosevelt have at the time FDR won his first Presidential election?

314. Where and when did Martha Washington make her only public speech?

315. President Polk willed everything to his wife, Sarah, but hoped she would do what?

ANSWERS

309. At Camp David, Md.

310. Anne Francis (Robbins)

311. After their visit Lucy & Rutherford Hayes banned liquor and wines from the White House

312. 20

313. She taught at the Todhunter School for Girls in New York and edited a magazine, *Babies—just Babies*

314. In Philadelphia, thanking her military escort and the public, while en route to New York, 1789

315. Divide the estate, on her death, equally between his and her blood relatives

316. Why was Lou Hoover so expressive in her hand movements during White House dinners?

317. What part did Mamie Eisenhower play in the romance of her grandson, David, and Julie Nixon?

318. What was the name of Dolley Madison's relative who married President Van Buren's son and acted as White House hostess?

319. Who hired financier J.P. Morgan's Swedish cook for the White House kitchen?

320. When was the term *First Lady* popularized?

321. Why did Helen Taft demand the dismissal of the U.S. Ambassador to France?

322. What did Lou Hoover feel about Prohibition?

323. Why did Pat Nixon's father call her Pat after he gave her the names Thelma Catherine?

ANSWERS

316. It was her method of giving orders to the attendant staff

317. She suggested that David, studying at Amherst, look up Julie at nearby Smith College

318. Angelica Singleton

319. Helen Taft

320. By journalist Mary Clemmer Ames reporting on the 1877 inauguration

321. During her honeymoon the same man had refused to get a special invitation for the Tafts—and she remembered

322. She did not remain at functions if liquor was present

323. He liked St. Patrick's Day, which fell the day after her birth

324. Who turned down Secret Service protection after an attempt on the life of her husband?

325. Why did Eunice Shriver stand in for Jacqueline Kennedy when the King and Queen of Afghanistan arrived?

326. Who kept open house every evening for informal gatherings at the White House?

327. What did Woodrow Wilson give his wife, Edith, for her 44th birthday?

328. This woman has been described as a smoker of corncob pipes.

329. Who was hostess during the Presidential term of widower Thomas Jefferson?

330. What famous collection began with the presentation of Helen Taft's inaugural gown?

331. How did Grace and Calvin Coolidge dampen wild rumors that they would divorce?

332. Why did Julia Gardiner refuse to marry President Tyler in the White House?

ANSWERS

324. Eleanor Roosevelt, in 1933

325. The First Lady was expecting her third child

326. Lucy Hayes

327. A platinum brooch

328. Margaret Taylor

329. Dolley Madison, wife of Jefferson's Secretary of State

330. The Smithsonian Institution's collection of First Ladies gowns, in the Museum of American History, Washington, D.C.

331. They appeared together more often in public

332. It reminded her of royalty which offended her democratic principles. They married in Manhattan

333. Why was the 22nd anniversary of the Japanese attack on Pearl Harbor so memorable for Lady Bird Johnson?

334. This First Lady's youngest son died in aerial combat over France in World War I.

335. For what destructive act is the only son of President Fillmore and his wife, Abigail, remembered?

336. Name the famous registered nurse who cared for Rosalynn Carter's dying father.

337. How did Dolley Madison's first marriage end?

338. Why did Lou and Herbert Hoover always dine alone on February 10th?

339. Before her marriage, this woman flirted with the man who later defeated her husband for a U.S. Senate seat.

340. Which First Lady got lost en route to Washington D.C.?

341. Who majored in geology at Stanford University?

ANSWERS

333. It was her first night in the White House as First Lady

334. Edith Kermit Roosevelt's son, Quentin

335. Millard Powers Fillmore ordered his executors to destroy all correspondence between his parents and himself

336. Miss Lillian, mother of Jimmy Carter

337. With the death of her husband, John Todd

338. It was the day they were married in 1899

339. Mary Todd Lincoln was wooed by Abraham Lincoln and Stephen Douglas

340. Abigail Adams - for 2 hours in the woods

341. Lou Hoover

QUESTIONS

342. How much older was James Madison than his wife, Dolley?

343. Why did Julia Grant order a West Point cadet put to bed in the White House?

344. Who was born Claudia Alta Taylor?

345. What was the name of the ship aboard which Abigail Adams first crossed the Atlantic?

346. What illness compelled Eliza Johnson to delegate the duties of First Lady to her daughter, Martha?

347. What did Congress give Helen and William Howard Taft on their silver wedding anniversary?

348. Who was First Lady at the centennial inauguration of a President of the U.S.?

349. Which First Lady was born in Boone, Iowa?

350. Who wore an old dress to the inaugural ball?

351. How did Dwight Eisenhower meet Mamie?

ANSWERS

342. 17 years

343. She learned he was freezing in her husband's second inaugural parade

344. Lady Bird Johnson

345. *Active*

346. Tuberculosis

347. The Senate presented silver compote dishes. The House gave a solid silver service

348. Caroline Harrison, wife of newly-inaugurated Benjamin Harrison

349. Mamie Eisenhower

350. Rosalynn Carter wore the same dress she'd worn to Jimmy Carter's gubernatorial inaugural ball in Atlanta, Ga. 6 years earlier

351. She visited friends at Fort Sam Houston where he was stationed

QUESTIONS

352. How long after JFK's assassination did his widow leave the White House?

353. Who cared so affectionately for her nonagenarian mother-in-law that the old woman called her *"my mother"*?

354. What was the first job Rosalynn Smith (Carter), 13, took after her father died?

355. Guess who wrote: *"French authors have occupied my attention the largest portion of my life."*

356. How many movies did Nancy Reagan act in before her marriage?

357. How did Pat Ryan receive her engagement and wedding rings from Richard Nixon?

358. Which First Lady said shortly after her husband's death: *"The story is over."*?

359. Who played hymn music on the White House piano after dinner?

360. Why did Edith and Woodrow Wilson graze sheep on the White House lawns?

ANSWERS

352. 14 days

353. Dolley Madison

354. She washed hair at a beauty parlor in Plains, Ga.

355. Louisa Catherine Adams, wife of John Quincy Adams

356. Eight

357. In a May Day basket

358. Eleanor Roosevelt

359. Lucy Hayes

360. So they wouldn't have to employ manpower to mow it during World War I

QUESTIONS

361. What is the most famous piece of furniture purchased by Mary Todd Lincoln?

362. Whose daughter was baptized less than 3 weeks after the mother became First Lady?

363. Julia Tyler was an accomplished performer with this musical instrument.

364. Jane Pierce implored her servants, for her sake, to do what once a week?

365. Where did Harry Truman first meet Bess?

366. How did Grace Coolidge react when her 6th grader failed in deportment?

367. Who was First Lady when the first reigning British sovereign visited the White House?

368. Who was called *Her Serene Loveliness* by a sarcastic newspaper writer?

369. What symbol did Caroline Harrison paint as her signature on her art work?

ANSWERS

361. The solid Rosewood *Lincoln Bed* in the White House

362. Rosalynn Carter's daughter, Amy

363. The guitar

364. Attend church services

365. At Sunday School in Independence, Missouri

366. She threatened to withhold his Christmas present

367. Eleanor Roosevelt, in 1939 during the visit of King George VI and Queen Elizabeth

368. Julia Tyler

369. A four-leaved clover

QUESTIONS

370. Which First Lady summoned her family to the table by trilling *"Famileeeee!"*

371. Who was the talk of the town for her 29-course dinners, with 6 wine glasses per guest?

372. The corpse of this First Lady's son was dug up by body-snatchers and deposited in a medical school.

373. What did Pat Nixon describe as *"the most relaxing part of the day"*?

374. Which elegant First Lady chose ivory silk taffetta and rosepoint for her wedding dress?

375. She was alone among First Ladies in serving as her husband's private secretary.

376. What color clothes did the aging Edith Kermit Roosevelt wear throughout the summers?

377. How much was artist Howard Chandler Christy paid for his White House portrait of Rachel Jackson?

ANSWERS

370. Lucy Hayes

371. Julia Grant

372. Anna and William Henry Harrison's third son

373. Breakfasting alone while reading the morning papers

374. Jacqueline Kennedy

375. Sarah Polk

376. White

377. $1,000

378. How long after the death of her son, Eddie, did Mary Todd Lincoln give birth to Willie?

379. Whose 6 ft. 4 ins. son was nicknamed *Prince of Washington* because of his playboy lifestyle?

380. A famous candy bar was named after whose daughter?

381. Which President's widow died while hearing a recitation from the Bible?

382. This woman learned German so she could help her professor husband with his research.

383. How was Julia Grant related to Russian nobility?

384. Who gave birth to her 7th and last child on Christmas Day?

385. Whose eyes were said to be clear gray but deepened to black when excited?

386. What was the native state of the first woman to live in the White House?

ANSWERS

378. Less than 11 months

379. Ellen Arthur's second son, Chester Arthur II

380. Frances Cleveland's daughter, Ruth, was known as *Baby Ruth*. After she died at age 12, the candy company renamed a bar with her nickname

381. Dolley Madison, in Washington, D.C.

382. Ellen Axson Wilson

383. Her granddaughter, Julia, married Prince Michael Cantacuzene, former Chief of Staff to Grand Duke Nicholas of Russia

384. Lucretia Garfield, 1874

385. Lucy Hayes

386. Massachusetts—Abigail Adams

387. What gift did Jacqueline Onassis give her husband, Aristotle, for Christmas 1968?

388. On whose lapel did Betty Ford mischievously pin a button reading *Keep Betty in the White House*?

389. Who regularly walked in the White House grounds with her husband after breakfast?

390. How many trees did Rosalynn and Jimmy Carter plant around the White House?

391. Where did Jacqueline Kennedy stage the sumptuous dinner party for the President of Pakistan?

392. Who was known in Europe as *La Belle Americaine*?

393. What did Israeli Premier Golda Meir give Pat Nixon on an official visit to Washington?

394. Which First Lady converted to Roman Catholicism 27 years after leaving the White House?

395. On what did Eliza Johnson spend most of her days in the White House?

ANSWERS

387. A small portrait of herself by Aaron Shickler

388. Walter Mondale's, while he was Jimmy Carter's running mate in 1976

389. Edith Kermit Roosevelt

390. Four, from Georgia: a Loblolly Pine, Red Maple, Plane Tree and a Dogwood

391. At George Washington's home, Mt. Vernon, Va.

392. Elizabeth Monroe, when her husband was U.S. Minister to France

393. An 11th century B.C. necklace of carnelian beads

394. Julia Tyler

395. A rocking chair

396. Who gave birth to an 11 lb. son?

397. Why was Rosalynn Carter barred from being chairperson of the President's Commission on Mental Health?

398. When fire broke out in her home she insisted on saving her husband's papers, at great personal risk.

399. In which country were John Quincy and Louisa Adams married?

400. Who gave birth to her only daughter on the Fourth of July?

401. Who ordered a replica of the 8 ft. 6 ins. × 6 ft. 2 ins. Lincoln bed for her husband on his retirement?

402. Why was Helen Taft a White House guest for several weeks while still a teenager?

403. What was the first gift Grace Goodhue received from Calvin Coolidge?

404. The closest confidante of this First Lady was a freed slave.

ANSWERS

396. Lucy Hayes, with the birth of Scott, 1871

397. She served as *Honorary* Chairperson because the law forbade a President from appointing his wife to a civilian position

398. Dolley Madison, who was rescued at 4 a.m. in the 1848 blaze

399. England, 1797

400. Julia Grant gave birth in 1855 to Ellen *"Nellie"*

401. Edith Bolling Wilson

402. Her father was a friend and law partner of President Hayes and she attended her sister's christening

403. A porcelain plaque of Mt. Tom, Vermont, which they had visited together

404. Mary Todd Lincoln

405. Which former First Lady died 2 days after her daughter's husband?

406. What did Bess Truman hold instead of a bouquet at her wedding?

407. Both Julia and Ulysses Grant made these mistakes in their writings.

408. How many times did Eleanor Roosevelt sit for her White House portrait?

409. Who wore a sealskin coat with a chinchilla collar to her husband's inauguration?

410. Who sometimes cut college classes to earn money as a movie extra?

411. When she married a President her wedding ring was fashioned from a gold nugget gift from the people of California.

412. How many countries did Rosalynn Carter visit on a trip to Latin America in 1977?

413. What was Lady Bird Johnson's favorite TV show?

414. This First Lady had an English nannie when a child, and hired one for her own children.

ANSWERS

405. Elizabeth Monroe - September 23, 1830

406. A prayer book

407. Spelling and grammatical errors

408. 12 sittings

409. Florence Harding

410. Pat Nixon, to help finance her studies

411. Edith Bolling Wilson

412. Seven: Jamaica, Costa Rica, Ecuador, Peru, Brazil, Colombia, Venezuela

413. *Gunsmoke*

414. Jacqueline Kennedy

415. What did Franklin Roosevelt usually call his wife?

416. What color did Bess Truman choose for her White House sitting room carpet?

417. How did Mamie Eisenhower pass long, lonely nights during World War II?

418. What was the name of Grace Coolidge's pet red chow?

419. How many of Helen Taft's 5 children survived?

420. Who was First Lady when a record million-plus tourists visited the White House in a single year?

421. What was Pat Nixon's favorite reading material?

422. She lived in 28 homes between marriage and the White House

423. Who had a narrow escape from death when her horse threw her on a tarred road?

ANSWERS

415. *Ma*

416. Plum

417. She read a lot of mystery thrillers

418. *Tiny Tim*

419. Three

420. Jacqueline Kennedy (1961)

421. Historical novels

422. Barbara Bush

423. Edith Kermit Roosevelt (1911)

424. What happened to Edith Bolling Wilson's only child, a son?

425. How did Grace Coolidge react to Charles Lindbergh's offer to take her up in a plane?

426. John Jacob Astor held a $6,000 mortgage on this famous lady's Washington home.

427. What was Eleanor Roosevelt's favorite flower?

428. As a child she was good at baseball, fishing, horse-riding, swimming and tennis.

429. What did Jane Pierce carry with her on an almost 2-year-long European vacation?

430. Why did Pat Nixon squat yoga-like in the Diplomatic Reception Room?

431. Why did Lucy Hayes have to cover up holes in the carpets with White House furniture?

432. What was the most popular name given by First Ladies to their sons?

ANSWERS

424. The child, from her first marriage to Norman Galt, died when 3 days old

425. She declined, saying she'd promised her husband she would never fly

426. Dolley Madison

427. A yellow rose

428. Bess Truman

429. A box with locks of hair from her deceased sons, mother and sister

430. She copied her guest, an instructor in self-improvement courses

431. An adversarial Congress had refused appropriations for White House running expenses

432. John

QUESTIONS

433. Where did Jacqueline Kennedy sleep her first night in the White House?

434. How did Julia Dent meet her husband, Ulysses Grant?

435. This President spoke admiringly of his wife as the *"polar center"* of his life.

436. What was suspended between White House trees for Helen and William Howard Taft's silver wedding anniversary party?

437. She never returned to Washington and never spoke of the White House during the 2 years she survived her husband.

438. Whom did Lucy Hayes invite to dinner every Thanksgiving at the White House?

439. How did Nancy Reagan get a bump on her head 2 days before her husband's re-election as President?

440. How much did the government pay for a piano Dolley Madison wanted for the White House?

ANSWERS

433. In the Queens' Room

434. Her brother was Grant's room-mate at West Point

435. Woodrow Wilson, of his first wife, Ellen

436. An arched, electric sign flashing *1886–1911*

437. Margaret Taylor

438. The clerical staff and their families

439. She forgot that the hotel bed was raised on a platform, and fell onto a chair

440. $458

441. Who consulted a fortune-teller several times about her husband's political prospects?

442. What did Ellen Wilson request of her physician the day she died?

443. This First Lady's son was Secretary of the Interior under Theodore Roosevelt.

444. During 4 years as First Lady she knitted more than 3,000 pairs of slippers for sale by charities.

445. What allowance did Mamie Eisenhower's father give her after the birth of her first child?

446. What did President Truman promise to give his wife if she tripped up Sen. John Bricker (R-Ohio) on the White House floor?

447. At what time did Mary Todd and Abraham Lincoln breakfast together?

448. Why did Betty Ford read her husband's telegram to victor Jimmy Carter after the 1976 election?

ANSWERS

441. Florence Harding, shortly before his election to the Presidency

442. To press upon the President that he should remarry

443. Lucretia Garfield's son, James

444. Ida McKinley

445. $100 a month

446. A pearl from the jeweled dagger presented by the Saudi Arabian King

447. About 8:30 a.m.

448. The President had laryngitis

449. Who refused to let her husband chew tobacco in public?

450. Which First Lady could converse in Chinese with her husband?

451. When Alice Roosevelt Longworth was pregnant, which First Lady did she confide in?

452. What kind of watch did Mary Todd Lincoln wear after her husband's assassination?

453. Helen Taft wore a feather from this bird at her husband's inauguration.

454. Where were Woodrow and Edith Wilson married?

455. Why did Florence Harding keep Pete in a cage?

456. This former First Lady attended the funeral of Egyptian President Anwar Sadat.

457. This future First Lady slept on the floor during a tour of Prussia with her husband.

ANSWERS

449. Florence Harding

450. Lou Hoover

451. Grace Coolidge

452. A *mourning watch* set in black onyx

453. An egret

454. In her home at 1308 20th Street N.W. Washington, D.C.

455. He was her pet canary

456. Rosalynn Carter

457. Louisa Catherine Adams, wife of John Quincy

458. What did Grace Coolidge do on learning that her husband had become President?

459. Why did Harry Truman agree to sit in the same car as Dwight Eisenhower after the latter refused to get out and greet him?

460. This widow of a President died on the anniversary of his birthday.

461. What did the wedding of Eleanor Roosevelt have in common with the marriage of her third son, Franklin Jr.?

462. What did Jacqueline Kennedy call her mother-in-law, Rose?

463. What did Pat Nixon request of Santa Claus at a White House Christmas party?

464. Which First Lady had pink roses placed daily in her bedroom?

465. This pipe-smoking woman died after her husband's election but before his inauguration.

466. With whom did Helen Taft replace policemen stationed at the White House entrance?

ANSWERS

458. She cried then knelt with her husband to pray

459. It was Ike's inauguration day and Bess Truman calmed down her husband

460. Edith Bolling Wilson died on December 28th, 1961

461. Rev. Endicott Peabody was the Minister at both ceremonies

462. *Belle-Mère*—French for mother-in-law

463. A diamond necklace

464. Mamie Eisenhower

465. Rachel Jackson

466. Liveried footmen

QUESTIONS

467. Name the three musical instruments played by Abigail Fillmore.

468. Who was First Lady when electric lights were first installed in the White House?

469. What was the total number of domestic and maintenance staff at the White House when Lady Bird Johnson moved in?

470. Who starred in a melodramatic home-made movie called *Heaven Will Protect the Working Girl*?

471. Thomas Jefferson was once the suitor of which First Lady's mother?

472. Why was Pat Nixon frightened, as a child, on her daily walk to school?

473. What kind of books did Bess Truman prefer to read?

474. What was the name of Martha Washington's childhood horse?

475. Her 1932 Christmas card was handwritten *"From Lou Henry Hoover, Weejie and Pat."* Who were they?

ANSWERS

467. Guitar, piano and harp

468. Caroline Harrison

469. 75

470. Lady Bird Johnson in 1942

471. Dolley Madison's mother, Mary Coles

472. She had to pass a grove of trees on the mile-long walk

473. Mystery novels

474. *Fatima*

475. *Weejie* was her Norwegian elkhound and *Pat* her German shepherd

476. Who was the youngest First Lady?

477. After wearing a $10,000 dress for one night this First Lady said she felt like Cinderella.

478. What painting hung above Mamie Eisenhower's White House bed?

479. Who campaigned to make corn the national vegetable?

480. Where was Pat Nixon's mother born?

481. How old was Quaker-born Dolley Madison when she was confirmed in the Episcopal church?

482. What was LBJ's birthday gift to Lady Bird, 2 weeks after moving into the White House?

483. Who got excited whenever she heard the sirens of fire engines?

484. How did Jacqueline Kennedy sign most of her memos?

485. Who held membership number 281,200 in the Daughters of the American Revolution before her protest resignation?

ANSWERS

476. Frances Cleveland, aged 21

477. Nancy Reagan, when she presented her inaugural gown to the Museum of American History in the capital

478. A woodland scene painted by her husband

479. Caroline Harrison, during her husband's Presidency (1889–93)

480. Germany

481. 77

482. His photograph, inscribed: *"To Bird, still a girl of principles, ideals and refinement, from her admirer, Lyndon B. Johnson"*.

483. Bess Truman, who once drove after fire engines instead of heading for the theater

484. *JBK* - (Jacqueline Bouvier Kennedy)

485. Eleanor Roosevelt

QUESTIONS

486. Who suffered from claustrophobia from childhood?

487. What colored materials did Martha Washington choose for her servant's uniforms?

488. How long after meeting Pat Ryan did Richard Nixon propose marriage?

489. What did Julia and Ulysses Grant nickname their son, Ulysses Simpson, Jr.?

490. Why did Florence and Warren Harding bring their own furniture into the White House?

491. This President gave orders that he *was* to be disturbed if his wife ever called.

492. Which First Lady became Mrs. Thomas Preston?

493. Who was addicted to TV soap operas?

494. What pet did Dolley Madison save from invading British soldiers?

495. What were the tasks of two Britons in Eleanor Roosevelt's employ in 1919?

ANSWERS

486. Mamie Eisenhower

487. Scarlet and white and orange and white

488. He proposed the first night

489. *Buck*

490. As an example of government economy they declined Congressional money for new furniture

491. Harry Truman

492. Frances Cleveland, who remarried after her husband's death

493. Mamie Eisenhower

494. Her green parrot, given to a servant for safekeeping

495. One was an English nurse, the other a governess from Scotland

496. How many years after her marriage did Mary Todd Lincoln die?

497. While being courted by a widowed President this young woman solicited autographs from Congressmen and Judges.

498. What did Rosalynn Carter major in at Georgia Southwestern Junior College?

499. Who designed Jacqueline Kennedy's gown for the state dinner at the Palace of Versailles, France?

500. How many of the 30 White House rooms had been plastered when Abigail Adams moved in in 1800?

501. Who began her autobiography: *"My mother was one of the most beautiful women I have ever seen."*?

502. Why did Mamie Eisenhower suspend skeletons from the State Dining Room chandeliers?

503. How much rent did Pat and Richard Nixon pay for their Alexandria, Va. apartment in 1947?

ANSWERS

496. Four months short of 40 years

497. Julia Gardiner, later wife of President John Tyler

498. Interior decorating

499. Givenchy

500. Only 6

501. Eleanor Roosevelt in *This Is My Story*

502. For a Halloween party for wives of White House staff

503. $80 a month

504. What was Bess Truman's reply when asked if a woman would ever be U.S. President?

505. Who scorned changing hair fashions and stuck to parting hers, drawing it down and coiling it at the nape of her neck?

506. This First Lady saw two of her daughters married in the White House before her death.

507. What day did President Carter regularly schedule for a weekly working lunch with Rosalynn?

508. What double catastrophe struck Dolley Madison in October 1793?

509. How long did it take to pack Grace and Calvin Coolidge's possessions when they left the White House?

510. Where did Helen Taft wake up on the day she was to become First Lady?

511. Where did Mamie Eisenhower live during most of World War II?

512. When she was a child she won the school shot put championship.

ANSWERS

504. A crisp *"No"*

505. Lucy Hayes

506. Ellen Wilson

507. Thursday

508. Her first husband and 7-week-old son died

509. 7 weeks

510. In the White House, as an overnight guest

511. In an apartment in the Wardman Towers, Washington, D.C.

512. Bess Truman

513. Who shocked society by inviting a jazz group instead of the Marine Band for her son's Christmas party?

514. Who studied White House history at the Library of Congress?

515. What jewels made up Frances Cleveland's engagement ring?

516. This First Lady insisted on fresh orchids and roses daily for the White House living quarters.

517. Why did Abigail and Millard Fillmore close the White House to visitors once a week?

518. Related by marriage, these First Ladies both celebrated golden wedding anniversaries.

519. At what age was Eleanor Roosevelt orphaned?

520. What manual work did Florence Harding do voluntarily during World War I?

521. Washington Irving described her as *"a fine portly, buxom dame"*.

ANSWERS

513. Lou Hoover

514. Lucretia Garfield

515. Sapphires and diamonds

516. Helen Taft

517. On Sundays they worshipped then kept the day free for rest and family

518. Abigail Adams and her daughter-in-law, Louisa

519. 10

520. With other U.S. Senators' wives she sewed clothes for war orphans

521. Dolley Madison

522. What prompted Nikita Khruschev to send a white puppy, *Pushinka*, to the White House?

523. These First Ladies were friends and gossiped during the 1929 inauguration.

524. Which First Lady drew criticism for driving regally with a carriage drawn by 4 horses?

525. How old was Nancy Reagan when she gave birth to her last child?

526. Did Rosalynn Carter wear a hat on the cold January her husband was inaugurated?

527. Who gave Jacqueline Kennedy her German shepherd, *Clipper*?

528. How heavy was the Taft's silver wedding anniversary cake?

529. At whose home did LBJ and Lady Bird lunch on his last day as President?

530. Where did Grace Coolidge prefer to sit when she went to the theater alone?

ANSWERS

522. Jacqueline Kennedy playfully requested one of the pups of Russian space dog, *Strelka*

523. Grace Coolidge and Lou Hoover

524. Julia Tyler

525. 36

526. No

527. Her father-in-law, Joseph Kennedy

528. 75 lbs.

529. The Washington home of his Secretary of Defense, Clark Clifford

530. Orchestra level, five rows from the stage

531. Where was Ida McKinley at the moment her husband was shot in Buffalo, N.Y.?

532. What did Betty Ford do with the room Richard Nixon used as his bedroom?

533. Why were Herbert and Lou Hoover, Quakers, married by a Catholic priest?

534. Why did Jane Pierce arrive in Washington only 2 months after her husband's inauguration?

535. What did William Howard Taft call his wife, Helen?

536. Who escorted Jacqueline Bouvier to President Eisenhower's inaugural ball?

537. Why did Abigail Fillmore stay in bed for several hours before White House receptions?

538. What was Pat Nixon's dress size?

539. What did Rosalynn Carter drink first thing in the morning?

540. Who had a pet raccoon named *Rebecca*?

ANSWERS

531. Resting at the home of the President of the Pan-American Exposition, Buffalo, N.Y.

532. She converted it into a sitting room

533. There was neither a Quaker Meeting nor a Protestant Minister in Monterey, Ca. so they sought one of her family friends

534. She had tuberculosis and was mourning the recent death of her son

535. *Nellie*

536. Sen. John Kennedy—5 months before their engagement

537. To rest her ankle, permanently injured in a fall

538. 8

539. A glass of orange juice

540. Grace Coolidge

541. How old was Bess Wallace when she married Harry Truman?

542. What was Martha Washington's childhood nickname, by which her husband called her?

543. Who was the first woman to witness her husband's inauguration?

544. In which White House room did Rosalynn Carter's mother always bed down when visiting?

545. Who ripped out identifying labels from dresses then gave them to a destitute woman near the White House?

546. What dual misfortunes delayed Abigail Adams from taking up her duties as First Lady?

547. Who had menus printed on white satin for her daughter's wedding?

548. How did Grover Cleveland become guardian of Frances Folsom before their marriage?

549. This First Lady entertained so often she had 3 assistants handle invitations.

ANSWERS

541. 34

542. *Patsy*

543. Dolley Madison, in Washington, 1809

544. The Lincoln Bedroom

545. Edith Kermit Roosevelt

546. The death of her mother-in-law and a freak spring snowstorm

547. Julia Grant, in 1874

548. Oscar Folsom and Cleveland were law partners. Folsom's will named him guardian of the girl, 11

549. Lou Hoover

550. How did Mamie Eisenhower campaign for Richard Nixon while Ike was hospitalized in 1968?

551. Her maiden name was Smith but she became one of the best known of all the First Ladies.

552. Soon after her marriage, this woman was asked to darn 50 pairs of her husband's socks.

553. Why was Mary Todd Lincoln terrified that her husband might not be re-elected President?

554. When was Julia Gardiner Tyler dubbed *Rose of Long Island*?

555. Who hosted a surprise party for Betty Ford's 58th birthday?

556. What memorial in Chaméry, France, did Edith Kermit Roosevelt finance?

557. This First Lady personally designed china plates for the White House.

558. What Southern dish did Rosalynn Carter include on the menu for her first state dinner?

ANSWERS

550. She handed out Nixon-for-President buttons at Walter Reed Army Hospital

551. Abigail Adams

552. Grace Coolidge

553. She had run up enormous shopping debts which she thought would have to be settled if he lost the election

554. Five years before marrying President Tyler and after appearing in an ad supportive of a Manhattan clothing store

555. Vice President Nelson Rockefeller and his wife, Happy

556. A fountain, in memory of her son buried there in World War I

557. Caroline Harrison

558. Shrimp Gumbo

559. What is the annual pension paid to Presidents' widows?

560. Why was Grace Coolidge's Secret Service bodyguard replaced?

561. On whose recommendation did Jacqueline Kennedy hire French chef René Verdon for the White House?

562. How old was Martha Custis (Washington) when her first husband died?

563. Who was "Miss" Allie Smith?

564. Which First Lady set aside a special room to display the White House china collection?

565. How many Presidential administrations did Edith Kermit Roosevelt live through?

566. When they first met she was impressed by *"the silvery sweetness of his voice"*.

567. Why were Abigail Adams' dresses damaged when she moved to the new capital at Philadelphia?

ANSWERS

559. $20,000

560. President Coolidge was angry when she returned 90 minutes late from a hike in South Dakota's Black Hills

561. Her father-in-law, Joseph Kennedy

562. 25

563. Rosalynn Carter's mother

564. Edith Bolling Wilson

565. 17 by the time she died in 1948 aged 87

566. Julia Gardiner, on meeting incumbent President John Tyler

567. Her suitcase was waterlogged when the ship sprung a leak

568. Who officiated at the wedding of Caroline and Benjamin Harrison?

569. Which First Lady lived the longest?

570. Which New York City museum was Pat Nixon's favorite?

571. What was the color of Abigail and John Adams' home in Philadelphia?

572. What did Grace Coolidge call her husband?

573. Why did Louisa and John Quincy Adams walk over dinner tables at the Lord Mayor of London's banquet?

574. About how much was paid annually in salaries to Lady Bird Johnson's press staff?

575. Who dropped out of Smith College after her freshman year to marry a future President?

576. Why did Jacqueline Kennedy move from Washington to New York City after the assassination?

ANSWERS

568. Her father, Dr. John Scott, a Presbyterian minister

569. Bess Truman, who was 97

570. The Frick

571. Green

572. *Papa*

573. Because throngs of people blocked their path on the way out

574. Almost $100,000

575. Barbara Bush

576. Persistent ogling sightseers outside her Georgetown home upset her

577. Where did Edith Bolling Wilson learn to ride a bicycle?

578. What two prohibitions did Florence Harding issue immediately after her husband's death?

579. What birthday present did Jimmy Carter give Rosalynn in their last year in the White House?

580. Who never charged anything she bought?

581. What was the average weekly number of letters received by Jacqueline Kennedy?

582. Who liked angel-food cake more than any other?

583. Before becoming First Lady this woman owned a fashionable Washington, D.C. jewelry shop.

584. Why did Lucy Hayes' parents leave their Presbyterian church and become Methodists?

585. Which First Lady wrote of Elizabeth Monroe that she *"moved like a goddess"*?

ANSWERS

577. In the White House basement

578. Bans on a death mask and an autopsy

579. A framed passage from the Bible: "*Live happily with the woman you love*....."

580. Bess Truman

581. 7,000

582. Eleanor Roosevelt

583. Edith Bolling Wilson

584. Because the pastor in Ohio was sympathetic towards slavery

585. Louisa Adams

586. How many years did Grace Coolidge live after becoming First Lady?

587. What were Lady Bird Johnson's favorite blossoms?

588. Which First Lady secluded herself in the White House and wrote notes to her deceased son?

589. Why did Florence Harding's father refuse to speak to her for years?

590. What was the crowd size outside the White House during the Taft's silver wedding anniversary party?

591. How did Julia Grant's father bail her out of financial hardship soon after her marriage?

592. Was Pat Nixon in favor of her husband running for governor of California?

593. Which of her predecessors did Jacqueline Kennedy admire most?

594. Whose mother read Greek, Roman and Teutonic myths to her when the child was only 5?

ANSWERS

586. 34 years

587. Peonies

588. Jane Pierce

589. He disapproved of her marriage to Warren Harding, in whom he lacked confidence

590. 15,000

591. He gave her a farm near St. Louis

592. No

593. Bess Truman

594. Lady Bird Johnson's mother, Minnie Taylor

595. Why was Edith Bolling Wilson furious at the inauguration of her husband's successor?

596. As a 3-year-old she cried watching Abraham Lincoln's funeral procession.

597. Which First Lady started the famed collection of White House china?

598. Where was Mamie Eisenhower when Ike died?

599. What cabinet portfolio was held by John Quincy Adams at the time his mother, Abigail Adams, died?

600. On their honeymoon this incumbent President wrote a poem and she set it to music.

601. Which First Lady was noted for her phenomenal memory?

602. What single exception did Lucy Hayes make to her refusal to accept silver wedding anniversary gifts?

603. When this President died his widow refused to let his body be embalmed.

ANSWERS

595. Because Warren Harding left the physically weakened Woodrow Wilson to go alone to an elevator

596. Edith Kermit Roosevelt

597. Caroline Harrison

598. Holding his hand in his hospital room

599. Secretary of State

600. President John Tyler and his second wife, Julia

601. Bess Truman

602. She accepted a silver plate inscribed *To the Mother of the Regiment* from her husband's 23rd Ohio Volunteers

603. Zachary Taylor's wife, Margaret

604. Name the first painting acquired by Jacqueline Kennedy's committee formed to redecorate the White House.

605. How did Pat Ryan (Nixon), 18, cross the continental U.S. in search of a job?

606. How long had Rosalynn Carter been married when she became First Lady?

607. What did Mary Todd Lincoln make sure her husband wore during their last winter together?

608. What dress size fit Nancy Reagan?

609. What was the name of the ship upon which Louisa Adams returned from England in 1817?

610. Why did JFK order the lights turned on in the car en route to the inaugural gala?

611. Who was the first American woman presented at the Court of St. James, England?

612. From which country did Mamie Eisenhower's maternal grandfather come?

ANSWERS

604. A 1767 portrait of Benjamin Franklin by David Martin

605. She drove an elderly couple in their Packard from California to New York

606. 31 years

607. His gray shawl

608. 4 and sometimes 6

609. *Washington*

610. So the crowds could see Jacqueline Kennedy better

611. Abigail Adams

612. Sweden

QUESTIONS

613. Which President often called his wife *Mommy*?

614. Which First Lady saw her daughter married in the same church she had wed in 37 years earlier?

615. This First Lady became a grandmother for the first time on Pat Nixon's 27th wedding anniversary.

616. Who walked her dogs around the White House grounds before bedtime?

617. What did Lou Hoover admit she would miss most as First Lady?

618. What did Jacqueline Kennedy place in JFK's casket in Dallas?

619. Who cried uncontrollably during her husband's inauguration?

620. Who died in the White House only months before the end of her husband's term?

621. This First Lady moved into the White House, fired the male steward and hired a female housekeeper.

ANSWERS

613. Ronald Reagan

614. Bess Truman, at the wedding of her daughter, Margaret

615. Lady Bird Johnson, June 21st, 1967

616. Eleanor Roosevelt

617. Having everything done for her by servants

618. She placed her wedding ring on his finger

619. Mamie Eisenhower

620. Caroline Harrison

621. Helen Taft

QUESTIONS

622. Who was best man at Jacqueline and John Kennedy's wedding?

623. This First Lady called her husband *"the dearest sweetest boy that ever lived."*

624. Her father, Marvin Pierce, was chief executive of the McCall Publishing Company.

625. Where did Martha Washington hang the small portrait of herself painted by John Trumbull?

626. Which First Lady preferred candlelights to newly-installed gas lights?

627. Who sometimes studied the stars from the White House roof?

628. Why did the press lambast Mary Todd Lincoln for her White House party?

629. What did it cost Julia and Ulysses Grant for the dinner in honor of Prince Arthur, son of Queen Victoria?

630. Who got a woven gold evening bag, with her initials in diamonds, from Saudi King Fahd?

ANSWERS

622. The groom's brother, Robert

623. Helen Taft

624. Barbara Bush

625. In her bedroom at Mt. Vernon

626. Sarah Polk

627. Rosalynn Carter

628. They disapproved of it being held during wartime

629. About $2,000

630. Nancy Reagan, during his State visit in 1985

631. Where was Martha Washington during her husband's first inauguration?

632. This woman was being wooed by an incumbent President when her father was killed in a freak accident.

633. Who did Rosalynn Carter invite to entertain at a banquet following the Middle East peace treaty?

634. Why did Dolley Madison sleep with a Tunisian sword near her bed?

635. Which First Lady got a diamond tiara on her silver wedding anniversary?

636. Who never attended the theater after the death of her husband?

637. Just married, this woman failed miserably in a cooking course.

638. What overall theme did Jacqueline Kennedy direct for her husband's funeral?

639. This future First Lady told her husband that George Washington had *"dignity with ease"*.

ANSWERS

631. At Mt. Vernon

632. Julia Gardiner married President Tyler 4 months after all 3 were aboard a ship when a gun exploded, killing her father

633. Opera singer Leontyne Price

634. The British were expected to invade Washington

635. Helen Taft, from President Taft

636. Mary Todd Lincoln

637. Mamie Eisenhower

638. That it should resemble Abraham Lincoln's funeral

639. Abigail Adams

QUESTIONS

640. Why was Woodrow Wilson received so joyfully at a World Series baseball game in October 1915?

641. Why did President Tyler reject Dolley Madison's request for a diplomatic post for her son, Payne Todd?

642. Which First Lady refused to allow trumpeteers to announce the arrival of the First Family?

643. What was the cause of Abigail Adams' death?

644. How many days did Mary Todd Lincoln remain in the White House after her husband's assassination?

645. Why did Mamie Eisenhower abruptly leave Pat Nixon's surprise 57th birthday party?

646. Which First Lady was born Edith Carow?

647. What did Ellen Wilson give her daughter, Eleanor, for a wedding present?

648. Guess Eleanor Roosevelt's favorite jam.

ANSWERS

640. He brought Edith Bolling Galt, to whom he had become engaged 2 days earlier

641. Because Todd was a renowned profligate and idle layabout

642. Rosalynn Carter

643. Typhoid fever

644. 38

645. To return to her hospitalized husband

646. Edith Kermit Roosevelt

647. Bedroom furniture

648. Strawberry

649. Who conceived the idea for a White House garden area where First Ladies could entertain?

650. Who wore black to her wedding and immediately became First Lady?

651. What custom relating to bed sheets did Eleanor Roosevelt change?

652. Who kept a scrapbook of her husband's activities?

653. This First Lady had bachelors degrees in arts and journalism.

654. Where did Grace and Calvin Coolidge honeymoon in 1905?

655. Guess the nationality of the man who called Bess Truman *"a good woman"*?

656. By what name did Pat Nixon answer phones at her husband's law offices?

657. What was Mamie Eisenhower's favorite White House room?

658. Who met Dutch Queen Wilhelmina and later described her as *"stupid"*?

ANSWERS

649. Jacqueline Kennedy

650. Edith Bolling Wilson

651. She ordered White House sheets changed
    twice a week instead of daily

652. Bess Truman

653. Lady Bird Johnson

654. Montreal, Canada

655. Soviet Foreign Minister Molotov during
    a World War II visit to Washington

656. Miss Ryan, her maiden name

657. The third floor solarium

658. Edith Kermit Roosevelt

659. Whose death was Grace Coolidge mourning when she became First Lady?

660. Which First Lady inscribed on her White House portrait: *"A trial made pleasant by the painter."*?

661. What did Lady Bird Johnson's father give her as a graduation present?

662. What musical instrument was Louisa Adams accomplished in?

663. What food did Mamie Eisenhower often send Ike in Europe during World War II?

664. How did Dolley and James Madison leave Washington at the end of his Presidency?

665. As a young lady she studied at the Art Students League in New York City.

666. Which First Lady departed the White House without saying goodbye to the staff?

667. Who chaired the United Nations commission which drafted a universal declaration of human rights?

ANSWERS

659. Her father's. He had died 3 months earlier

660. Eleanor Roosevelt

661. A trip to Washington, D.C.

662. The harp

663. Packaged noodle soup

664. By steamboat down the Potomac River to Aquia Creek

665. Ellen Wilson

666. Helen Taft

667. Eleanor Roosevelt

668. On being married to a politician, this woman said: *"It's a hard life."*

669. Name the first couple to celebrate a 25th wedding anniversary in the White House?

670. What were Bess Truman's favorite flowers?

671. This future First Lady worked briefly in a New York City X-ray laboratory.

672. Who lived in the house which was later home of Stanford University's president?

673. This woman received flowers from her husband every year on the birthday of their deceased son.

674. For which newspaper did Jacqueline Kennedy report Dwight Eisenhower's 2nd inauguration?

675. How did White House staff refer to Eleanor Roosevelt?

676. How many people were on Betty Ford's White House staff?

ANSWERS

668. Pat Nixon

669. Lucy and Rutherford Hayes, 1877

670. Yellow roses, red tulips and all azaleas

671. Pat Nixon, in 1932

672. Lou and Herbert Hoover

673. Mamie Eisenhower

674. The Washington *Times-Herald*

675. They called her *Mrs. R.*

676. 26

677. How much did Congress vote to give Dolley Madison for her husband's private papers?

678. What time did Martha Washington normally go to bed?

679. She financed her husband's first campaign for Congress with an advance on an inheritance.

680. What was Jacqueline Kennedy's reading material a few weeks before becoming First Lady?

681. What did Julia and Ulysses Grant give their future daughter-in-law for her marriage to their son, Frederick?

682. What was Rosalynn Carter's favorite place in the White House?

683. Who kept a diary as First Lady but refused to write a book?

684. Why did Abraham Lincoln's secretary call Mary Todd Lincoln *"Her Satanic Majesty"*?

685. What was eerie about the Willard's Hotel room where Abigail Fillmore died?

ANSWERS

677. $30,000

678. After her husband, about 10:30 p.m.

679. Lady Bird Johnson

680. Books on the White House

681. A pearl necklace

682. The Truman Balcony, overlooking the Washington Monument and Jefferson Memorial

683. Pat Nixon

684. He insisted on inviting the beautiful wife of a cabinet member to a state dinner, over the objections of the jealous Mrs. Lincoln

685. It was the same room where her husband, Millard, succeeded to the Presidency 3 years earlier

686. Whose speech was impaired after a stroke in her first year as First Lady?

687. This First Lady's son raced his bicycle around the White House East Room.

688. A week before dying this former President visited her grave and said he longed to rest beside her.

689. Which celebrity millionairess was a close friend of Florence Harding?

690. Which First Lady was married on New York City's Fifth Avenue?

691. Who had piped-in music to all the bedrooms at her ranch home?

692. When was Jacqueline Kennedy inspired to give gifts of American minerals to foreign VIPs?

693. Who went alone to the inaugural ball?

694. This President and First Lady were both children of Presbyterian ministers and first met in church.

ANSWERS

686. Helen Taft

687. Lucretia Garfield's son, Irving

688. Rutherford Hayes, who was buried beside his wife, Lucy

689. *Washington Post* owner, Evalyn Walsh McLean

690. Julia Tyler, in the Church of the Ascension

691. Lady Bird Johnson

692. On a visit to the Museum of American History

693. Eleanor Roosevelt, in 1933, after FDR cancelled his appearance

694. Woodrow and Ellen Wilson

695. What did New York socialites covet during Martha Washington's term as First Lady?

696. How did Edith Bolling Wilson get sprayed with champagne?

697. What did Julia Grant frequently forget to wear before receiving guests?

698. This First Lady had no formal education but was an intellectual and taught herself French.

699. Who was so popular that it was estimated she alone would help capture about 10 percent of the electoral votes?

700. What prompted President Tyler to quip: *"They cannot now say I am a President without a party"*?

701. What did Lady Bird give LBJ for his 58th birthday?

702. Why could Jacqueline Kennedy not have the horse given her by the Pakistani President as the riderless horse for JFK's funeral?

ANSWERS

695. Invitations to her Friday night receptions

696. Christening a ship during World War I

697. Either her gloves or earrings

698. Abigail Adams

699. Mamie Eisenhower

700. His wife, Julia, invited 2,000 guests to a White House party

701. A 19th century wooden sailor's chest

702. It was considered too unmanageable

703. Who scolded her husband for wanting to retain *"an absolute power over wives"*?

704. The sister of which First Lady eloped with George Washington's nephew?

705. Why did a U.S. Navy commodore give Julia Tyler an Arabian horse?

706. With what drink did Jimmy and Rosalynn Carter celebrate their wedding anniversaries?

707. Whose son testified in court that she was *"of unsound mind"*?

708. Who received a basket of spring flowers from President Ford on her 90th birthday?

709. What did Thomas Jefferson's teen-age daughter have to say about Elizabeth Monroe after her stay at Monticello?

710. What gift from President Wilson did Edith Bolling Galt wear at their wedding?

711. Why did Pat Nixon, born March 16th, customarily celebrate a day late?

ANSWERS

703. Abigail Adams, in a letter to him 3 months before signing of the *Declaration of Independence*

704. Dolley Madison's sister, Lucy, 15, in 1793

705. President Tyler had bailed out of trouble the officer, who had illegally shipped horses on a U.S. ship

706. Champagne

707. Mary Todd Lincoln's son, Robert

708. Bess Truman

709. Daughter Maria pronounced her *"a charming woman"*.

710. A diamond brooch

711. When she was born her father returned home after midnight and called her *"St. Patrick's babe in the morn."*

712. What were Grace Coolidge's favorite wild flowers?

713. Which First Lady raised money for southern mountain women by exhibiting their hand-made rugs?

714. What was the estimated cost of gifts given Julia Grant's daughter, Nellie, for her wedding?

715. How long after becoming First Lady did Jane Pierce, mourning the loss of a son, attend receptions?

716. At what age did Edith Kermit Roosevelt become First Lady?

717. Who petitioned the Senate for a pension pleading she could not *"live in a style becoming"* a President's widow?

718. What color were Martha Washington's eyes?

719. Who narrated Aaron Copland's *A Lincoln Portrait* on stage in the nation's capital?

ANSWERS

712. Gumbo Lilies and Shooting Stars

713. Ellen Wilson

714. $60,000

715. Nearly two years

716. 40

717. Mary Todd Lincoln

718. Hazel

719. Rosalynn Carter

720. Which First Lady died the same day a bridge over the Potomac River was dedicated in her husband's name?

721. What size dresses did Lady Bird Johnson wear?

722. The serialization of this First Lady's autobiography boosted monthly sales of the *Ladies Home Journal* by almost 100,000 copies.

723. Why was Armistice Day, 1918, filled with sorrow for Mamie Eisenhower?

724. What was the value of Edith Kermit Roosevelt's estate?

725. How old was Eleanor Roosevelt when she became First Lady?

726. What was Bess Truman's height?

727. How long after JFK's death did his widow re-marry?

728. At which New York City hotel did Pat Nixon stay immediately before moving into the White House?

ANSWERS

720. Edith Bolling Wilson, on December 28th, 1961

721. 10

722. Eleanor Roosevelt's *This Is My Story*, 1937

723. She attended the funeral of her sister, Eda, 17, who died of kidney disease

724. $414,000

725. 49

726. 5 ft. 4 ins.

727. Five years

728. The *Statler Hilton*

729. Which First Lady was renowned for her flamboyant feathered headdresses?

730. How did Bess Truman invariably express displeasure with her domestic staff?

731. Who was First Lady when a swimming pool was built in the White House?

732. What food did Lady Bird Johnson offer Richard and Pat Nixon before setting out for the 1969 inauguration?

733. Guess what Ronald Reagan gave Nancy on their silver wedding anniversary.

734. Which President called his wife *"a good scout who knows all my faults and yet has stuck to me all the way"*?

735. Why did Pat Nixon cancel plans for new White House china?

736. How long after Dwight Eisenhower met Mamie were they married?

737. Who suggested her husband mention the American Family in his inaugural address?

ANSWERS

729. Dolley Madison

730. She was noticeably silent

731. Eleanor Roosevelt

732. Toast, sweet rolls and coffee

733. A canoe named *TruLuv*

734. Warren Harding, when introducing his wife, Florence

735. She felt it inappropriate as the Watergate outcome neared

736. Nine months

737. Rosalynn Carter

738. Guess which First Lady gave a visitor breakfast of sliced tongue, dry toast, bread, butter, tea and coffee?

739. What did Edith Bolling Wilson wear on her dress the first time she dined at the White House?

740. Who was married at the Mission Inn, Riverside, California?

741. Who belly-flopped in the pool then tried again to show her husband she could dive?

742. How old was Jacqueline Bouvier when her divorced mother re-married?

743. Who said *"I just want to go down in history as the wife of the President."*?

744. How many tiers were on the wedding cake of Lady Bird Johnson's younger daughter, Luci?

745. What was the annual pension drawn during the 27 years Julia Tyler survived her husband?

746. How old was Dolley Madison when she returned to live in Washington?

ANSWERS

738. Martha Washington, in 1794

739. Her favorite, a purple orchid

740. Pat Ryan Nixon

741. Eleanor Roosevelt

742. 12

743. Pat Nixon

744. 14

745. $5,000

746. 69

QUESTIONS

747. What is Eliza Johnson best remembered for?

748. Guess which First Lady wrote: "...*power and high position do not ensure a bed of roses.*"

749. Which First Lady lived at 21 Massasoit Street, Northampton, Mass.?

750. How many guests attended Jacqueline and John Kennedy's wedding reception?

751. What was Bess Truman's favorite color?

752. What was the profession of Dolley Madison's first husband?

753. How old was Eleanor Roosevelt when she was widowed?

754. This First Lady invited friends to china-painting classes in the White House.

755. Why did Mary Todd Lincoln ban flowers from the Executive Mansion?

756. Who admonished her son, a U.S. Senator, never to dress shabbily?

ANSWERS

747. Teaching her husband, Andrew, to write

748. Mary Todd Lincoln

749. Grace Coolidge

750. 1200

751. Blue

752. Lawyer

753. 60

754. Caroline Harrison

755. Because her son, Willie, had liked flowers, and he died in the White House

756. Abigail Adams

757. Critics scorned this First Lady for being seated on a raised platform during receptions.

758. How many miles of travel, alone, did Lady Bird Johnson clock in her first year as First Lady?

759. Which recent First Lady refused to serve liquor in the White House?

760. This First Lady was so popular that Congress almost banned manufacturers from exploiting her picture on their products.

761. What did Eleanor Roosevelt invariably suggest when FDR asked what she wanted for Christmas or her birthday?

762. Why did a healthy Mamie Eisenhower move into a hospital for 11 months?

763. What did Helen Taft arrange for the public the night after her silver wedding anniversary?

764. What was Abigail Adams referring to when she wrote she had *"a limb lopped off"*?

ANSWERS

757. Julia Tyler

758. More than 45,000 miles

759. Rosalynn Carter

760. Frances Cleveland. Legislation introduced in the House of Representatives in 1888 was not passed

761. Linen or anything she could *use*

762. To be beside her ailing husband in 1968

763. She let them walk around illuminated White House grounds while being serenaded by the Marine Band

764. Her husband sailed for France as a U.S. Commissioner and took along their son, John Quincy, 10